iWrite
Words & Voices

Original Poetry by

Jason Brain
C.R. Cohen
Sean Hill

POETRY IN MOTION
PUBLISHING HOUSE

CHAPBOOKS IN THIS COLLECTION INCLUDE:

Part I
iWrite
Collaborative Chapbook

Part II
Words & Voices

Singing in a Thunderstorm
C.R. Cohen

Thoughts of a Lost Dreamer
Jason Brain

Love is/in Life
Sean Hill

All Written Works and Revisions
by Jason Brain, C.R. Cohen, & Sean Hill

Organized and Designed by Jason Brain

Cover Art & Design by Gina Concklin

Poetry In Motion Publishing House
Los Angeles, CA

Copyright © 2014

ISBN-13: 978-0991605309
ISBN-10: 0991605306

All Rights Reserved

No part of this publication may be reproduced or transmitted in any form or by any means, electronic or mechanical, including photocopying, recording, or by any information storage and retrieval system without the prior written consent of the publisher.

First Edition - 2014

*To all the Poets & Philosophers, past and present:
Who would we be without you?
Namaste*

JB

*To my husband, Ari, whose unshaking
belief and support make it all possible.*

CC

我所有的中国朋友。我经常想起你。你影响我永远.

*Each one of us, of this planet, to that part of us, small or
large, waning or intensely vibrant, that believes we will
achieve universal realistic inner & outer world peace in our
lifetime … this is to, for, and because of you.*

SH

Part I:
iWrite

iWrite

Muse
Lost Midnight Memories, The
Peel The Pain
Dream Zombie
The First Poem
Petals On The Altar
The Invention
City Lights 2013
How I Got Here
I Dream
Write Now … Like Now … Ok?
History Copy(right?)
Haiku I
Fail!
The Inspiration Boom
Chrysalis Of Night
This Is A Poem
This Poem …
Poem
Where The Wild Things Are
Mind Body Purpose
Between Lying Down & Falling Asleep
Worlds Within … Universes
In Case Of Ego
Not The Masterpiece
I Am Your Poem
Still Finding Stillness
Wild, Wild Western
Free Write To The World
#ThinkOutsideMyBox
No Words For You
Literary Theory II
No Voice
S(U)perheroes
The Mission
These Words Mean Something

JB   CC   SH

 Muse

A wisp of greatness
Brushed past my mind yesterday
While I was busy counting coins
For the parking meter
On an Ocean Avenue street corner

Brushed right past me
I stood
Too awe-struck then
To react
Not quick enough even
To extend the arm and clasp

And so it floated by
And it was gone

It sounded like a whisper
And lured like a siren
Taunted like a vixen
And left me like a mistress

Sweet sultry Muse
Revisit me in dreams
These daily waking nightmares
Seem at times
Near bearable
With the promise of your form
Which stalks my door

You leave me static
Afraid to turn away
For fear you shall return

You trap me here within
Your prisoner, held captive
A slave to gossamer inspiration
Pale light refracted
Upon the mist of fading genius

If not for you I could perhaps
Be happy

Lost Midnight Memories, The

I had you in the late lay me down
Misplaced you in the early morning rise

Desperately striving for where you've flown
The thoughts, I thought, I thought I'd had

Ones, floating upon midnight clouds
In silent starlight, twilight to the sky

Sun gazing to find out what's so unknown
Suffering, forgetting all that's so sad

Peel The Pain

Some perspire
To inspire
Sweating life
Out pores
Desperately
Overcomtemplating
When there are already plates
Of seismic inspiration
Swelling within
Ebbing
The ocean
Of life
Residing within
Bubbling anciently
Like billion year old brontosaurus bones

Reach
Deep, feel all the way
Into depths
Of fathoms
Of what
Who you think
You are to find out
What is truly
Under all
These layers

Even

Enjoy the pain of peeling

Dream Zombie

It scares the shit out of me
I continue to trust

Missing, mourning
Former incarnations of self

Hopes, Dreams, Aspirations

Sometimes it was a silencer
To the back of the head

Sometimes Louisville slugger-style
And a 3-foot shallow grave
In a cornfield

Tidy or messy
But always gangster
Always unexpected

A million little deaths
Murders
Suicides
The one thing I never learned to do was die

Defying logic is what dreamers do
Defying science is what artists do

We are the fucking zombies
Of the creative world

A million little deaths and we keep coming
Feeding off Life and never dying
Knocked down
Back up
Relentless
Again and again
And a-fucking-gain

There is no bullet can lay us down

The First Poem

So I'm reading this silly poem, drinking tea in some coffee shop
Don't know exactly who sold it to me but he seemed very nice

Said he was selling love in paperback for only three bucks
I gave him five

I open this napkin he sold me and begin reading
Wondering if this could be the first poem he's ever written
Fuck, it's probably the third poem he's written with this title alone

It's called
The First Revolution
And it goes a little something
Like this:

"Get up!
Do you hear me?
What are you waiting for?!
Dance!"

Now I'm sitting here, wondering
What if everyone in this room was reading this poem, too?
What if, at the same exact time, everyone looked around
And immediately got up and obeyed?

Would you put the poem down and follow the leader, too?
Who doesn't like to dance?

Nobody leads if you do it right, so
What's stopping you, love child?

Get up and go, or
Stay down and follow
But always choose
To dance

There's music
In the poetry
In the despair
Of daily life

Petals On The Altar

Thoughts
Scattered

Like a thousand rose petals
Upon the altar of lost ideas
Upon the disconnected
Disjointed
Upon fleeting genius that does not come

Many brilliant but disparate pieces
With potential to become a whole

Something beautiful

Yet some days those thoughts remain rose petals
A thousand tiny prayers
Sacrifices to the Muse

That the gods of inspiration
Might alight upon us again

The Invention

Of inventing

Venting relentless
Stress or seductive
Happiness releasing
Honesty in bursting
Fashion or slow
Steady streams
From brushstrokes
To backstrokes
Synchronized anything
Rhythm relays
Passionate displays
Of inner workings
Inner playings
Inner everything
Inner anything
Wanting
Needing

Out

City Lights 2013

In City Lights
A poet's mind
Ignites with
Meta-revolution

Dancing in quiet
Between aisles
Arms up
Eyes ablaze

The history of Beat
In the air and wood
We breathe in
Brother's skin
For the first time
Lungs blessed
Holding our breaths
As if this may be
The last time
Poetry is
Inside of us

The view from the attic
Desolation in the basement
Fuck everything on the 1st floor
Fuck everything outside

We take our time because we want to
There's nowhere else we'd rather be

One mustn't rush fingertips down spines
One can never be rushed to write
One never hurries to revise

Young poets
In City Lights
San Francisco, CA
One soul
Resides

How I Got Here

I lined my pockets with hopes and dreams
And left my logic vacant
Lived on credit and unemployment
Ramen and Kraft inspiration

Running years
On fumes of faith
On dangled carrots
And twice-crossed fingers

I held my breath
Held tight, held tough
I held hands with the Devil and God

We all sang a round of Kumbayah
But the campfire eventually blotted

Came darkness
Came silence
Came avoidance of self

Came a blinding light of brilliance

Rebirth can happen to anyone
And when it does
We write a poem

 I Dream

Some days I want to scream at the sky
Just to hear that my voice can do it
Some days I want to run with all might
Just to feel that my legs can bear it

Some days my heart beats strong
With an aching feeling that recognizes
We all want these things

Yet we follow the rules
And we sit still
Stagnant, silent

But I hold to the knowledge
That these feelings inside me
Mean I'm still alive

I dream of pastures and echoing chambers
Of wide open spaces
And beams of sunlight
I dream of grand adventures

I dream of Europe and of cafes
Of underground taverns
And worldly discussions
I dream of revolution

Let the wine and spirits flow
Let the conversation flow
Let the passion and quarrels flow
Let the inspiration flow

Let our hearts be full and open
And let us reach for more
Let us seem ridiculous
To all those who've stopped dreaming

For how can you have a dream come true
When you don't even have a dream?

Write Now ... Like Now ... Ok?

This is what it's like

Either spontaneous overflow
Or methodical thought
In a state of tranquility
Or not

Either it gets expressed
All at once
Bits at a time
Or not

Either you share it
You don't
Or not

Either you criticize it
Or not

Either you feel better
After doing it
Or not

Either you end up realizing
How great it is to simply do it
Without judgment
Without past pain
Without comparison
Or ...

No

You will eventually realize it

So write

Now
Stop reading this
I'm serious
Just 10 minutes
Just write

Right now

(Uh, why are you still reading this?)

Go
Please

Don't look around
Like someone is watching you
Talk with this book …

Skedaddle

And maybe send me what you wrote …

If you want …

Or not …

If you don't want to

But writing … definitely do that

Or I'll poop

On your soul

… I've done it before

(It was an accident though)

History Copy(right?)

Everything is carbon
Copied over
And over

Nobody
Nor mind
Knows
Exactly
How old
How young
An essence
Truly is

Simulacrum

Another copy
Of another copy
Of another
Remembered
Recorded
Forgotten

For not

Haiku I

Nostalgia Informs
Elusive Inspiration
Poetry is Born

Fail!

This is no longer poetry
I don't recite lines
Designed to entice minds
These poems morph
Into monologues
Impactful speeches
Aimed to teach without teaching
But now that I said that
I may have backtracked
And backfired my own goal
In letting you know
How I hope to "trick you" …
As if that's what this is
Thick with rabbits
Top hat magicians have tried
That and more
So from the first to the last chance
I need to
I would love to
Dance inside your mind with you
Then shrink wrap, package
Postage pay, send, and forward you
Universal truth to live by
Between that
And sharing stories
To catharsis this existence
No longer shall audiences think artists
Have to or want to
Jump through hoops
To entertain
To entertain
Are you not entertained
By life already
Best special effects just looking into space
Plus we live on a floating rock
With a trillion cells inside we get to tell what to do
Breathing 23,000 times a day of O2
With choices that have infinite potential
And you
Want an artist to make you feel good
When you forget how to

Well here it is, rest your expectations forever
1: We are human before entertainer
2: You can be the bold artist of life you already are
3: You have everything you need
4: It's better to make a mistake
Than to have never started what you set to accomplish
And 5: Remember, we are working on all this
Just as much or more than you are as an audience

This section is specifically towards
Those who give
The appearance of listening
The appearance of giving attention
Limiting their connection
To themselves and others
While giving claps of respect
Because you would never get up here
And speak your mind
Defend it, open it, get it rear-ended
And still manage to afford to get it fixed up again
No insurance to buy
For peace of mind
Premium rates doubled since the last war on error
Because being wrong
Seems to be the first non-stop flight on any guilt trip
When last I checked my checked baggage
It said on the tag that, "the best lessons learned come from failure"

So please, fail
Let's *all* fail
Fail at something you love or something you don't
Just fail greatly

I want to fail SO good with you

Make so many mistakes
We can toss them in a lake
Chase each other to the nearest ocean
Where we reach in after the rocks
To observe how rocks & waterfalls have beaten them
Into beautiful patterns of forgiveness
And after the failures mingle with seaweed
We dive in, bathe, and play in these waters
Of failure in order to understand & absorb each other better

Let's fail so hard
Scars look like future lesson plans
Where our own bodies teach us
How to be better selves
From sincerely
Studying & healing
Our scar tissue illusion

Let's fail so beautifully
So
Honestly
That we can
No longer hide or use lies
Because truths
Will become the easiest thing to say
We'll realize we're not saving anyone
From any pain anyway
Usually it's just a delay
And we'll learn the best way
To say anything we need
From a heart
That's mindful
Present
And considerate
Consider it

Done

As soon as you
We
Decide to

Be

Successful

At epic

Failing

The Inspiration Boom

It's a boom that becomes a bang
Shakes up, breaks down everything around
It's the words that are nothing more than air
Written in hot breaths beneath the shadows we despair

Above all the rest
Life's the true test
We just leave dust
Run over the cusp
And find the sounds
You wish would come down
And fill you with found
In the exhales lost
In the silence left
Unsaid

Better off dead?
No way!
Didn't you hear what I just said?

Fucking find it
Take it in and write it
There's no time to
Do, think, say, and rue
So let it out
Breathe it in
Just as deeply
Without sigh

The boom is gone
But what has it left behind?

Silence only seems so wrong

Walking around
People keep singing the same damn song

On and on and on and on

Chrysalis Of Night

Find in night a solace
A peace not elsewhere found
An echo chamber
A cavernous maw
Inwardly folding towards your own raw perceptions of self

The most private thoughts blanketing
Reflective with familiar hum
As the whirring of a space heater
The guttural song of the feline purr

Embrace the you inside the chrysalis of night
Pure and unbetrayed
In this single moment of you
That will never again exist
Save within the words upon the page
And the memory of forming them

And knowing that this moment
Stitches in time with identical moments
Of the past, of now, of future
To form the same moment in the collective consciousness
That in this moment
We are one

This Is A Poem

What is poetry?
It isn't beauty feeling so soft and shiny
It isn't lovely words sounding all pretty-like
Poetry just is
What it is

Do you hear me?

She's a metaphor
A faberge explosion
Different than before, she is
A newfound heartfelt emotion

Every moment I fight, I rise, I die
Every time I'm brought back to life
From the womb of writer's block

Do you feel me?

I hope so, because
Everything you say, think, do, and not
Becomes your own poetry
In motion

The answer comes, though
Through which direction
Your question is going

And just like poetry
I am, is, are, was, were

And just like myself
You are, too

And just like yesterday
We're gone

And just like tomorrow
We're not

This Poem ...

This poem is a thank you
This poem is not original
Above all
And below all
This poem is

This poem was not made in China
It was made
In love
Which is everywhere
This poem is not your friend
It's your best friend
It's always there for you
And will play video games with you
Even if it's a one player game
(Cause you do the whole
Let's-beat-the-game-by-switching-every-level-thing
Which is fun to do if you both like the game ...)
This poem may get sidetracked
This poem is that kind of friend
That will tell you the truth
No matter hard it is to say it
It knows what's best for you
Like your mom
Or a good doctor
Or your God
Or the universe
Or whoever and whatever you think actually knows
What's best for you
Yeah
And that's only because this poem is you
And whatever you want it to be
But it's also what you can't control it to be
This poem is ... pretty ... deep
This poem is 4G, wireless
And won't make you go over your minutes
This poem is love
So if you love this poem
You love love
And everyone says
You have to love love before you love yourself
So, if you already love this poem, good job

This poem needs to do its laundry
This poem loves to do random things
This poem is what she said
This poem just became catchy
This poem doesn't rhyme for those of you wondering ...
This poem is a dream
Since you probably will remember
Only bits of it later ...
And maybe not at all
This poem is you
This poem has a crush on you
This poem wants to take you out
This poem wants to treat you right and get to know you
This poem wants to be inside of you
This poem might be moving too fast
By reading this poem
This poem is actually
Inside of you
This poem might not always be right
... Or is it?
This poem isn't afraid to ask questions
This poem doesn't care much about who is right or wrong
This poem does care if you're happy or not and why
This poem wants to work with you
This poem wants to know about your childhood
This poem doesn't like to use the word "never" or "always"
This poem ... has never fallen in love
Never
It always steps into it, holds its breath
And practices swimming in it whenever it can
This poem can be hypocritical if you look for it ...
And not ...
If you don't
This poem is not political
This poem is not an activist
This poem is not sponsored
This poem is not saying it's bad to be sponsored
This poem remembers all the things you call mistakes as lessons
This poem is reminding you to do that thing you're putting off
This poem enjoys pushing you forward, urgently, comfortable
Sometimes uncomfortable
You don't have to take this poem personally
But it would be nice if you did
But only in a good way
This poem is not meant to offend, commend

Attack, or defend, it said it before …
This poem simply is
This poem has perspective
This poem has experience
This poem is sharing
This poem is free
This poem is truly free
Free in the way ideas and words can fly without baggage fees
Free in the way one use to walk different lands without passports
Free like filtered, healthy water used to be
Free in the way hugs are
This poem is like the world
This poem is not perfect
But it can be if we all want it to be
If we all worked to agree on solutions by priority …
Maybe …
This poem already is perfect and the world is too
This poem is perfect in it's imperfections
Because it wants to be imperfect
Hmm …
This poem is saying a lot
This poem doesn't know everything
This poem likes to think
This poem likes not to think too
It likes self control and when to let it go
In a controlled way
This poem knows how not to think
Just by going … ( ) …
This poem is kinda silly
This poem can go on and on and on and on and off
This poem genuinely cares about everything that makes you *you*
This poem hopes you're not annoyed yet
And if you are …
This poem hopes you would expand your attention span
Beyond what you wished it could get
So you wouldn't miss anything life would give you
Not a single regret
Of a safe or unsafe bet
Where every moment that comes
Is a new exciting person you just met
And you give a willing and cheerful goodbye
To every moment that just left
Where every scene is critically acclaimed
In the movie of your life …
… Where you ask yourself …

Did I do everything I wish I could have done

This poem knows ...
You would absolutely
Without a thought ...
Say
Yes

Poem

Thoughts to share and words to shout
My mouth can't seem to get them out
Give me a pen with lots of ink
And I will tell you all I think

Where The Wild Things Are

Read me a story
Don't just feed me a plot now
Give me some words
Pass on to me a new thought, but
How?

The world keeps spinning
All and in throughout me
The sound of your breathing
Fills my body, my soul, my being

I imagine impossible spectacles
Phoenixing in full flight
Highly improbable situations
Metamorphosizing at midnight

This isn't about creating new words
Only changes in deceiving
I want you to read me a story
I live to sleep sound in silence still believing
The worst things in the world
Wait lying under my bed, and
A teddy bear's all I need to pull me through
The nightmare fight falling asleep
Inside, I writhe

Where tucked within my dreaming head
I exhale softly under twilight

Kissed on the forehead
Lullabye'd into fantasies
Of an honest reality
Or so it may seem

Don't believe in
Everything you read

Mind Body Purpose

Body
Sick with a fever
Screaming to halt
To sleep
Praying to the mercifully lazy
Not so

Mind
Numb with exhaustion
Lost days
Days turning somersaults
Rolling through weeks, through months
Driven

Sanity
Static, electric
Faltered
Shaken and unhinged
A threadbare blanket
Untucked

All
Caught up
Tumbled along with time
Not stopped to breathe, to break
Push through

Vault
Run up against your own ambition
Drive against drive
Urge upon urge
Body, Mind, Sanity
Protest
Disbelieve their limits
Disprove them
Disagree

No rest for the purpose-driven
No rest for the living

Between Lying Down & Falling Asleep

Brilliance doesn't just happen
All the time

Like lightning
It only touches down
Once in a flash

Never when you're ready
With pen or paper
At right hand, but always
When you're driving at night
Four in the morning
Swerving steadily in your lane
Steering with your knee
Writing on your left wrist
The last thing you just thought
Before it's lost, all gone

Oh, those beautiful lines
You were never to have found until now
But brilliance comes subtly
Tired and half asleep
On auto pilot in the mind

Every word rings of gold
So sublimely unkind, because
Now it's time
To revise

Who wants
To wake up
To that?

Worlds Within ... Universes

We have a second life

Within this one

Even more
With each step of new awareness

New worlds
With different gravity
A whole lot less
Almost floating with lightness

Enlightenment involves
One
To lighten up a bit

Leaving a light footprint on this planet
So my tracks won't wear it out

Plus the best road trip
Is inside

My travel agent
Is awareness

My passport is my will to understand
My visa never expires

My new job is oneness: it's always hiring
Anyone all of the time if you just give
It a little bit of your infinite

No overtime since time doesn't exist

Music is motion, vibrating life
Moving to my inner theme song
Beating in the key of G

The soundtrack I play to my verse
Where every moment is a surprise

So why, why would I ever close my eyes

This world was meant to be seen

Meant to be lived in
Meant to be received

Meant to be shared
Meant to be believed in

Meant to be witnessed
Meant to be kissed
Cared for
Connected to
Meant to be our mentor
Our friend

This universe was simply

Meant to be breathed in

By
Our
Uni
Verses

In Case Of Ego

Speak to someone smarter
Read something better
Try something harder
Push

Check your bank balance
Check your body of work
Check your trophy case
Strive

In case of ego, remember
You can always do better
Be better
Live better

Look forward and repeat the words
… And still so far to go …

Not The Masterpiece

I know it's good
I just did it

Certainly ain't nothing new
May be cool now, but what about soon?
Or a little later? How about then?
Will it still be cool then?

Because, really, what is art, anyway?
Beautiful? Bullshit?
What is love truly?

I know this ain't no kitsch, though
This isn't a rearview mirror on a walking cane, no
This is something meant to be seen

Tasted upon the eyes
Smelt with the ears
Felt inside the soul

Is this something meant to be sensed and believed in
Or is this something best left deep within my dreaming?

I don't care if it's cool
Nor do I care if it's hot, dope, rocking, awesome, killer, or nice

I just want to know
Could this be a classic?

I know it's not a masterpiece
But that's not what I'm asking

Could this be a classic?
I guess, in the end, we'll never really know

I really think it could be
You tell me

Want to see?

I Am Your Poem

A poem does not have to be a few pages long
In fact, it doesn't have to be one sentence short, either
It can be anything the poet prefers really; nothing is crime
You can do as you please; hell, you can even rhyme if you like

If this paper had a camera
It would shutter as you read it
And would you really be reading
If I was waiting so patiently by your side?
Would you tell me the honest truth
If you knew I were alive?

Are your passing eyes hearing me now, or
Are you merely just listening and nodding

This may be a poem and I may never know it
But such is the life of a poet, you know?

Heh, wouldn't you know it
You may understand it
But it can never be shown
It is an imaginary toy
A make-believe ploy
To bring back to you far away places
Places you may have never been before
Places you say fuck this, no more anymore
Places you play until you can't breathe no more
Places you may or may not have seen or been before
Yet still resonate in the way your body feels
Under the weight of gravity alone
This is friction

It's only a few words of diction
It's a slight of hand and some needed revision
This is friction
And it moves things

This is a poem
And I am a voice

And I
Move things

Still Finding Stillness

This is for the lessons just learned
For the lessons unlearned that burned us

This is for the new you
Happening everyday
The old you
Who had no idea what to say

For the unfinished sentences
That say so much
The metaphors that say more
Than intended
But still say what you aimed for

For all the time spent on wordplay
To find out that no amount
Ever adds up to an amazing quality of store-ray
And on-is-stay

For the friendships that have turned tides
Which may wash again on your shore
While facing that beautiful oceanfront

Remember the feeling of the sand you're standing in
It's sanding away the past you've walked in

Exfoliating the weight
Of the path you've traveled

While anchoring you
To a present

That is made up
Of tiny moments

Scattered upon your toes

So you can walk
Gently
And lovely

Sweetly

Or
Urgently

Into every new step
By step
Day by day

This is for every TV show title that applies to real life

First Boy Meets World
Or even if you are a New Girl

Breaking Bad until good times

And as much as you may wish for a Modern Family
When you get so upset and ask Who's The Boss
Just to end up in an Arrested Development
Really close to being Six Feet Under …
You can get Saved by the Bell …
Appreciate the Price is Right
Back when you were pulling out Weeds
As chores and weren't bored multiplying Numb3rs
To get good grades, not be slave to an Office
But rather a good addition to your Community
And not some crazy Animaniac

This is for the insomniacs
That maybe haven't yet tried
To truly let sleep come to them

For all the times we think we have to chase dreams
Whether they be American, pipe, lucid, or vivid
And think we have to hurt
Violate, oppress, resent, condescend
Patronize, manipulate, confiscate
Confuse, over-contemplate
Constrain, control
And simply, utterly, overpower …

When in fact …

Many of the most beautiful things
We have ever accomplished …
Many of the most lovely feelings
Ever felt …

Many of the greatest moments
Of peace

Have come to us ...
By simply

Being

Still

Wild, Wild Western

I pack a .357 Magnum
Manufactured by Bic
Shoots ink, blood red
And my shot's as sharp as shit

I say I'm deadly accurate
And you don't want to question it
'Cause I'll fire holes through all your bullshit
Won't even bat an eye

With fingers and keystrokes
I'm pounding down your door
To catch you with your pants down
In your dirty-secrets bedroom

There's no hiding from the words
This cowgirl slings

Free Write To The World

This is my free write to the world, alright?
There's no time for stopping until I'm finished, alright?
This is a free write, alright?
Let's go

I don't know if you know this or not, but
We live in one fucked-up place
Nothing remains homeostace, to create is a waste
I am no revision and that is my decision, my conviction
I only stutter-step when second looks won't do, it's true

Only circles repeat themselves around here, and
I'm a square: I don't care

Bitch, I have more sides than an nth-ahedron
I have more gusto than the world's longest run-on
I have all the time in the world until the last second's all gone
And then all that's left is on and on and on
On standby

Someone had to do it
There's no more time to pause
Momentum reiterates forward motion
Flowing in any direction
It's not a question
There is no answer
This is just a free write to the world, alright?

And I would have gotten it to you faster
Had I not edited in the in-between
Meta-morpha-sizing thought
Before wraught

I am no ones
Final draft

Like jazz
I am

To be
Do be
Do

#ThinkOutsideMyBox

Some look for inspiration
Like it's a god
They need to be saved by

Some think
They need to be
In a certain mood to write

I know this guy named
WAKE UP
Who just called you

Twist the angle of your scope
Find something in this room
You never noticed
Take a breath and hold it
Until you can't breathe
Exhale your past criticism
Take a fresh breath in
Taken less for granted
See the optimistic incisions
Waiting to be sliced
By the only you
In all of time
That will ever exist
Ever
Every breath
Makes you brand new
Every breath
You are
Brand new
Every breath
Breathe
Brand new

No Words For You

I, being poet
Often felt guilty

No words for you

Could never ink my thoughts for you
My urge for you
My feel for you

For words are static
A moment in time

Words don't move the same

This feel is ever-changing, flowing
The words just won't keep up

So I'm sorry I never wrote you
I'm sorry I never could say

It's just that a poet has a hard time admitting –

For you, there are
No words

Literary Theory II

Easy to tell a story, but
Tough to solicit true meaning
A deceiving imagination's believing
Easy to say what you please, so please, elaborate
Speak only exactly everything you mean

In the cosmic fabric of things
What once was only one centimeter
Can become one million miles in a snap

It's all relative
Depending
On how you look at it
So what're you looking at now?

What's catching your eye?
What is this you call life
Not just what you're doing right now?
And why?

It's easy to tell a story, but then again, it's even easier to lie

What are you saying?
I don't understand
How do you not understand?
I completely understand

I'm a madman in poet's clothing

It's easy to tell a story, but then again
It's even easier to tell a lie

It's easy to say you're truly living, but then again
It's even easier to truthfully lie

It's easy to stay ignorant forever, but then again
It's even easier to roll over and die

It's easy to tell a story
It's even easier to write non-fiction

But why?

No Voice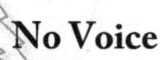

I sing no songs, not anymore
The tune is gone away
My days are dry
And stale as toast
My stagnant world of silence

The heated air that bakes my skin
The flies are 'round my head again
Reminding me I'm dead

These days are droning on and on
I, zombie, walk the earth

I am a hollow, am a shell
My stomach churns with emptiness

I make me sick to write these words
Like being forced to smile
A dried-up pen
A muted voice
And dry-heaved words upon the page
Thoughts wrung from a still-dry sponge

I am not writing from my head
Not with my heart or from my gut
I am writing from a place
That has no true existence

These words, they are invisible
These words, they have no meaning

These words are not attached to me
I am not attached to me
I've gone away
I gone away
And left a zombie in my place

My life is droning on and on
Where is the voice?
Where is the song?

Where is the fervent pen and brow?

It all has gone away somehow

My soul is gone
There is no calm
There is no quiet
There is no peace

There's only silence – no release

If I could but have the strength to cry
I could, but I've already died
Felt even not the pain of that
I cannot feel, I cannot write
I cannot write, I cannot right
Myself
I know I cannot right
The song is where?
The voices, where?
They wear and wear and wear and wear …

S(U)perheroes

Bigger than life beings

I aim at inspiring

Just nearly as much

Or much more

To set similes soaring

Like capes in the wind

Make metaphors matter

Like mystical or multiple dimensions

Commit actions impossible

Show they are normal

And save every individual

m o M E n t

Make sure each one is fully lived

Full of passion and self-expression

Able to leap doubt in a single bound

Enable us all

Remind us all

To be our own

Superheroes

The Mission

I lay
Years ago
In the swampy dank jungles of Vietnam
Limbs dangling from my body
Beaten
Battered
Bloody
And I crawled out
Inch by inch
I did
I did not wait for someone to come pull me out
No one ever comes

And if they do, they will only point the way
They will not carry you
No one will shoulder your burden for you

Your weight is too much to bear

I crawled my way out of my jungle
I alone have the power to put myself back there

I stand beside the veterans of this war
The ones who've made it out
And stand valiant
Triumphant
Beside me
These alone I stand with
These alone can point the way
They do it with honor
With pride

These are the marching orders of our mission

Stand shoulder to shoulder with these soldiers
Do not grieve the loss of those not ready
You have too much to do to get tripped up with them
And it is not fair to the others waiting

Will there be peril?
Yes
Will there be dark times ahead?

Absolutely
But will it be that which will deter you?
Will it be beyond your dealing?
Never
Your capacity is broader and deeper
Than they led you to believe it was

Your voice is the voice of the artist
Who fights against the masses
Fallen prey to mediocre existence

Sometimes enemies come
Let them come
Your life will be all the richer for your triumph over them

Brush them aside as you would the crumbs after a meal
For that is all they amount to

There is much work to be done

These Words Mean Something

These words
You speak
They do so much more
Than mean what they seem

Letters
Syllables
Grammar
Syntax

Lined up in fragmented structures
Guilty by association to everything else around

Where can one sentence send you to?

Inspiration
Conceptualization
Questioning
Realization

Schemas for the memories experienced
Dreamt up in your mind's own reality remix
What do you know, anyway?

Belief
Deceit
Truth
Relief

You are so much more than you seem
A fleeting being with other places to be
Other things to see, other emotions to feel, yet
To me you are just a name, a smile when you're happy, and
A frown when the days are a little more crappy, and
Unless you tell me something to really rock my socks off
You're usually exactly the same
A human being bleeding

I wanna see you in a new situation
Go back in the dressing room and try on a new life

I wanna see you in an old spectacle

Where you run for miles, bare-butt naked
Anything except a destination in mind

I wanna see you in real time
I wanna see you, so beautiful, in real life

I see you in my dreams
I see you in my dreams
I see you in my dreams, but
I've been daydreaming
For three days straight

My eyes may be closed but my mind's still going

I know you know, but
What do you mean, though?
Definitions don't include the word they're trying to define

A rose is beautiful because … why?
Find the words
They dance on your tongue
Loaded, ready to explode

Take your time
There's no need to rush

There's no such thing as a stupid word
Only stupid feelings

Find the words you know you want to use
Explain exactly what you mean

But first, before you do, remember
To breathe

It's the last thing you get
Before you're gone

Make it deep

Speak up

Part II:
Words & Voices

Singing in a Thunderstorm
by C.R. Cohen

Who But the Artist I

Attic

Not Guilty

Moth to Flame

Who But the Artist II

Beatnik Femme Fatale
Part III

Storm

Who But the Artist III

Confidence

Morning/Mourning

Haiku II

Who But the Artist IV

To The Ones Who Make You Feel Alive

Like Smoke & Honey

Who But the Artist V

Who But the Artist?

I

I dreamt of Colors, Light and Fragrance
                                Love and Passion. Dreamt.
I wasn't sure where I was going
                    Wasn't sure but cracked wide open,
      Knew that I exist

            I walked on ceilings
                      Was not told not to
            Strung words never pattern laid
                            and did not think it odd to

I called vanilla purple and beauty undefined
                      I tickled with my words
                    I opened with my words
                          Brought lightning with my words

          Tongues rolled velvet 'round my lines
                    My phrases kissed at lips

Corners upturned the mouths of men
                      and eyes, drawn shut,
                                  unclosed

       I grew up topless
                Danced at gravestones
                          Sang songs at full lung

I whispered words inside your head
                    to everyone's applaud

The words, the shapes, that your mouth makes
                        The rhythmic rhyming tongue

Discarding Decent, Obligation,
                    Duty-bound and Good

For I don't care much what you think,
                    except you say I should

Attic

Secrets run like shadows
Musty, moth-worn, molding
Begging not to be betrayed
By light of day
                or memory

Not Guilty

I let my morals get the best of me
   They want me to be good
                            So I oblige
Censor
      Edit
            Redact

These names have been changed
to protect
         the guilty

Be squeaky clean, they say
         File the serials off your sins
Sink misconduct in a lake
        Ignite vices in a flaming bonfire

Don press-on ties and petticoats
Walk in one straight line

They caught me
     with my mischief
              'round my ankles

Don't worry though
        I'll be better
                    next time

Moth to Flame

Ever the moth to flame
I was drawn again to your fire
My short-term memory was never that keen
(Never tangle with a devil in the dark)

But it was your white-hot poker
In shape of forked tongue that reminded
(It could burn and brand alike in equal measure)

I've slain many dragons in my day
But never one as vicious
Or as beautiful as you

Who But the Artist?

II

       Rabbit holes
              Rabbit holes
My mind has jumped to rabbit holes
                My mind has jumped through rabbit holes
      My mind has jumped for good

      I'm standing in a darkroom with a filmstrip
                                unexposed
I'm standing with a filmstrip,
          I think I'm meant to ruin

      Deep fissure down the heart of Art,
              deep fissure down Creation

A score-line scratch right through it all
              I'm growing large
                  I'm growing small

     So Eat Me. Drink Me. Fill me up.
            Pass the cake and pass the cup

Yet, Cheshire Pussy smiling wide
      while Hatter danced a tune

This Wonderland has ravaged me
                This wonderworld: Reality
    Thrust outside the Dream

Beatnik Femme Fatale
Part III

    my words hit you between the eyes
        I execute you with my truth
                with your truth
with the truth you've been a fugitive from for way too long
the way I was a fugitive from for way too long

    bold as a midnight moon
        vibrant as a blood-soaked crime scene

    I've read you backward and forward,
            yet you're standing still
I know better where you've been and where you're going
                  than you do
    I known the deviations you're too afraid to make
        the ones that'd save your life
my prayers are with you that you'll make,
              shake,
                  take the shift
and find yourself a life that makes you happy
            truly happy
a life that satisfies you deep within

                I'm speaking to myself again
    I'm speaking to the world
I have about as much faith in the world
        as I have in myself
            I scare the shit out of me at times
I execute myself in silence
    I give myself a voice
            I wonder when I'll be truly happy
Is it human nature to never be satisfied with where we are?
                or is it just me?
    I want to tell you I'm just like you
            truth is, I don't know
    are you as impatient as I am?
are you as disgruntled, dissatisfied as I?
        smiling through your frustration
gritting your teeth between enjoying the moment and settling
    unsure at times of how to tell the difference
        is it worse to pipe dream or to stop dreaming?

      to try and never make it
           or to never try and make it?
                suddenly life is a compromise
                        suddenly life is for someone else
         show me a time when it wasn't

                I want to believe I'm just like you
        I want to believe I'm normal
              or rather that we are all of us crazy
          crazy inside, normal world outside
the silent assassin, this invisible killer,
                  seeped within our veins.

    all of us crazy

everyone screaming like internal bleeding
      from some long-gone accident we keep forgetting
         working its way inside us
    permeating our innards while we look, we feel so normal
turn around and end up dead
            didn't even see it coming
the antidote:
        Live
              for what brings the passion
              what brings the fire
              in whatever way you can
        Live
              the rest is just a living
              the rest is just survival
              eventually, it's death

              I, for one,
                      choose Life

Storm

The sky was grey and steel blue
the air heavy-laden with moisture
a tangled dance of branches in trees

And it both thrilled and terrified
that the darkening gods were preparing
to open up and consume

There is anger and unrest today

The Heavens seek to wash clean of the Earth
all the ill and vicious behavior of the populace

We take cover,
lingering in bed clothes,
behind heaters and mugs of coffee,
staring out at the gail-soaked sky,
the impatient leaves whipping to and fro
like wisps of hair
around the vixen face of the siren,
a beauty who seeks to destroy

There is danger in the air today

Feminine naked form stands erect
feral, fertile before me
breasts and bush virginally ripe and seductive
yet solidly at odds with desire

They will not be taken

The length of chestnut-bronzed hair
extends from root to thigh,
straight and sensual
this form: a symbol of want and the forbidden

And the storm outside is the same,
existing in a time and place otherworldly
not of night or day,
pocketed in an immense void of solitude

The storm reminds us of ourselves,
always stirring impatiently
underneath the surface

There is the exhuming of uneasy feelings today

Now and again only so often
do we stir up our own emotions,
like leaves in the storm,
venturing,
daring to feel
a little of what simmers beneath,
the unrest that there resides,
aching for a riot,
throbbing for our own torrential downpour,
yearning for that we were the storm.

Who But the Artist?

III

Chains
          Chains I will not wear

The world and all those in it
          Step willingly into their chains
     Proffer bleeding wrists to chains
          Do not even see their chains

     The free man is the madman
          The free man laughs aloud
The free man dances in the street
          Runs up and down and 'round the street
          Strips naked and runs through the street
     Which one of us is smiling?

Who knows what Life is?
          Who knows what Art?
     Who, if not the Artist?

     One day

     One day was the first day

One day, an artist did something   different

One day, a brave   "Behold!"
          And people did
     Yes, they beheld
          Yet they could not see art

     But Hypocrisy and Death came in
          and called Van Gogh a genius
Called the Artist *brilliant*!
          Called *beyond his time*

     Who but the Artist?
          Who but the Mad?
Who in this world is smiling?
          Who is truly free?

Confidence

Today I walk a surer foot
No longer screaming but booming
No longer forcing but facing
Looking life in the eye
Challenging with no longer a scowl
But a smile

There is something to be said about Confidence
You do not earn it
You take it
That I've had to learn the hard way
Waiting long and vehemently for
Someone else
Someones else
To give it to me

Confidence
Is not something you are given
You do not find it
You have it

Confidence is not a thing
Hiding behind a rock
As if a golden Easter egg
At someone else's party

It is not won in some raffle
Because someone pulled your number
Nor is it something you've been saving up for
That you can finally buy

Confidence is something that you have
Because you demand it
You command it
It is not elusive like the fog
But a solid, stark and brazen
A shining, lightning thing –

That changes everything.

Morning/Mourning

The morning opens up slowly to me
And I once again recollect
Where I am and what has become

The time of refuge has passed along with the night
And consciousness rising tends things to surface
A shroud of heavy desolation covers me,
Darkening every corner of the room

A room that used to be ours

The day is a series of routines and habits –
Frequent presented examples of normalcy
Anchor recollections at bay –
It is repeated action and distraction
That keeps me moving forward

The nights are easier somehow
Alcoholism is a dissolving of sharp edges
Into nimbus halos of tolerance,
To bearing the contradiction of reality and the past

You will not be forgotten
But at least with something
Stiff and strong and amber,
Neither will you be so deeply felt

Still it is mornings when I remember most

Haiku II

People, like music
Verses are all different
Chorus is the same

Who But the Artist?

IV

        And the question remains
Where am I going?   What am I doing?
    The answer,   resolute
                  Exploring
                              I am exploring

Tripping down rainbows,
            dancing between lightning bolts
                    and laughing to the madness

Laughing at all the chainfolk,
                who feel calmed to call me mad

The shouldn'ts, the mustn'ts, the isn'ts, the wasn'ts
                    The miles and miles of dead
    The miles and miles of stop signs
            But miles above our heads

    Look there!   The Heavens!
        And look there!   The Horizon!

And once, for all, and finally
                Look there!   Inside
                    The Heart

Dancing in a lightning storm
              Singing in a thunderstorm
                    Screaming in a hot rainstorm

      Being none but me

To The Ones Who Make You Feel Alive

This is for the ones who know you
In all your glory
And all your ridiculousness
Better than you know yourself

Who would call you up
To tell you a story from their day
Just because it reminded them of you

Who, in telling that story
Will tell you something of yourself
You never noticed but was *so true*

This is for the ones who notice

This is for the ones who know your ambitions

To open artist centers around the world
To live and be alive in the world
To make a bold impact on the world

For the ones who know your dreams

To open minds
To touch hearts
To explore

This is for the ones who know your secrets

That you used to drink pickle juice from the jar
That you make up silly songs and dances
That you cry at the drop of hat
On the beauty of the human condition

Your bad habits

That you procrastinate
That you sleep too much
Have a multi-tasking addiction
That you're a closet slob and pack rat

And who love you anyway

For the ones who share your journey

Who else would go on that
Stealth slip 'n' slide mission
At midnight
In the middle of the apartment courtyard
After too much marshmallow vodka

This is for the ones you're rooting for

Because they're doing it
And they inspire you
'Cause they are doing what they want to do
Every single day and they are killing it
And because when you watch them doing it
You are doing it together

This is for those ones

Because they show up
All the time
Every time
Even when no one else does
Just to show they care

This is for the ones you live for
And the ones you can't live without

This is for the ones that make you feel more
You

Like Smoke & Honey

my thoughts, like honey, flow over you
thick, sweet, slow
licking across form and shape
expression and emotion

words, sounds
like tendrils of smoke
drifting along insides of mind

your eyes
speak soliloquies
too passionate to utter aloud

your mouth
cupping and caressing
desires, desserts, delvings

my breath snakes along
the grazed curve of your neck
tender sensation
delicate fingertips dancing across
surfaces as yet untouched

we come undone
unfolding, melting, thawing
palm against palm
against wrist
against elbow
ankle, knee
hip joint

against pelvic bone
and abdomen
lips

against soul

my mind wraps around you
your words, your gaze, your passion

the way yours wraps around me

Who But the Artist?

V

The freedom of flight

I've flown before   I've sailed before
    The freedom of Time and Space

        But someone told you Finite
                Someone said "an end"
Someone put up stop signs

    Someone, my darling,   lied

        Shatter

All could shatter to a million pieces
                But fear holds it in place

    Desperation clings to sameness
                in a lost and manic way

Hooked and scrabbling fingers
                clasp onto the cloth of Time

Draw repetition as comfort-shroud
                over blindness called a Face

        Eyes: unpurposed
Ears: unpurposed

    Touch and smell and taste unpurposed

Life was not a spiraled light

                It shall be once again

Thoughts of a Lost Dreamer
By Jason Brain

Dirty Romantic

WHY NOT?

In the Music

Scar Stories

Love Disease

Dreaming Behind the Wheel

POETRY COPTER

SWING

Kiss Me (Between Blinking)

Speak To Me

Why I Can't Wake Up At Six In The Morning

Last Takeoff

Untitled (Re-Vision)

To My Unborn Wonder

Dirty Romantic

I'm a dirty romantic

I fall in love too easily with the architecture of back alleys
I live amongst the treetops, tower over skyscrapers at sunrise
I dream from the womb of the oxygen in my near future
And there's nothing anyone can do about it

I'm a dirty romantic

Dancing for rain naked through midnight streets
Blowing etheric smoke rings nag champa
I am revolutionizing the art of breathing deeply
And refusing, refuting any rumors I've gone hipster

There's no greater threat to our way of life than corporations
And hipsters

Call me what you will
Except hippie or hipster, because
I'm a dirty romantic, and you
Don't have a death wish

I practice dirty romanticism daily
Don't get in my way; that's a warning
I've got waves to make, tides to carry away
All semblance of hope lost, in humanity found
Swimming against the rip to get close to my shore

I'm a dirty romantic

Not even my parents could do anything about that

You've been forewarned
I'm coming for you
Prepare yourself for my love

I'm a dirty, dirty romantic

Tell me
How do you like it?

WHY NOT?

I just wanna watch every sunrise
I just wanna dance anytime there's music on nearby
I just wanna love every lady leg that breezes by my way
I just wanna love my lady like the first time, every time
For the rest of our lives together

I just wanna be a man
I just wanna be a mans man
I just wanna be a ladies man
I just wanna be a man other men, women, little children remember
Long after I've become dust let loose to the wind

I just wanna burn
I just wanna leave nothing behind
I just wanna punk rock-it all the fucking time
I just wanna unapologize

I just wanna blow your mind
I just wanna fuck your sex
I just wanna graze your neck, bubble you in goosebumps
I just wanna powder you in mist from within
Then leave your lungs breathless for another 60 minutes

I just wanna love you
I just wanna love me, too
I just wanna love to love
I just wanna love to be loved like you

I just wanna be a little wiser than yesterday
I just wanna be a little better the next opportunity I get
I just wanna make our little world a worthwhile place
To raise my daughter in, and
I just wanna watch every sunset

I don't think that's too much to ask for

Why?

I just wanna

In The Music

When the music's loud
And when the music's good
And when the music's good and loud
There's nowhere else

Out of your seat, out of your mind
When it's good and loud and it's got you
There's nowhere, no one, no, nothing else
That matters

Turn me on
Turn it up
Let it loose
Let me in on
The magic

One foot to the ground
The other anywhere else
Both hands inside the ether
Hips infused to the wind

I burn with desire
A spark amongst the fire
Hold a flame in place for one moment
It's impossible, not really logical
Audience unstoppable
Why leave now?

When the music's good
And when the music's loud
When the music's got you
And you've let go
Completely
Willingly
There's only one question left

So ...

Care to dance?

Scar Stories

9 stitches
4 fractured bones
1 concussion
6 separate instances, and
A whole lot more to go, I am
Only getting started

Walking at 8 months old; I was on the move
Ready for adventure, a young man's legacy left to prove
Not two months later, running about
I tripped—hit my head on the VCR corner hard
Found myself with 2 stitches, gushing blood
A third eye lighting bolt from that moment until this one
I'm talking about scar stories

Speaking volumes more than any iTunes collection or vacation photos
Who knows where we'd be without these tales of the flesh
During moments in elevators without anything to talk about
How awkward without a scar story in your back pocket

How sad how simple, how safe your life would be

Get hurt
Know pain

There will come a day you only wish you were still alive
Waking up once again in the after light
Hell without action, every moment unknown
Taking chances by the throat

We note the fact of these happenings called accidents
There's a whole world daring us to keep pace, follow after
But we never knew no better than the chase
As we uncovered the Mohs of blacktop asphalt
The unforgiveness of gravity
Hypothesized the breaking point of human flesh, then
Went on to discover how many licks it takes
To get to the center of connective tissue

My body has stories to tell
Some more unbelievable than the scars will admit
They're humble like that

They help me remember myself sometimes
Every time they come to mind
Remind me
Moreso, than vacation photos or iTunes collections
I am more than memories
I am resilience

In every ounce of opportunity a pinch of danger
But that's why we like it, right?
Life, living, love, losing

No matter how many times we fall
We fall
And we get up once again
Dying to feel weightlessness once more
Staring into night skies so deep
We need the starlight
To keep grounded

Tell me about
Your most gnarly scars
Visible or not

I'd like to get to know you better
Through tales of your sacred temple
Not your measly day job or today's weather
I want to experience touch together
Let skin meet skin

You have a tale to tell

Where do you begin?

Love Disease

If eye contact were a disease
You'd swear I'd be HIV

I can't help it
I need to see you
The shine of your pupil
The light inside your mind
I need to feel you
I can't fake it
Communication
Otherwise

Let's hold right there
Where attention stands ready
And neither end will let go

Let's hold right here
Standing attentive, steadily
Clinging to this moment
Unspoken

If eye contact were a disease
You'd swear I'd be
Dead by now

I contracted an infection
I refused to be cured of
Whatever you do, beware
Vampires roam everywhere

I'm the last thing you see coming
Until it's too late

Don't wait too long
It only takes a glance
Before you know it
You're already gone

Was it good for you?

Great
Bye

Dreaming Behind the Wheel

I dream of the day smiles shine brighter
Laughter becomes currency
Dreams manifest into reality, and
I finally catch my breath

I dream of the day sons are allowed to be themselves
Daughters are comfortable in their own skin
Parents live to raise their children
Not the other way around

I dream of the day complete strangers become comrades
Families sit together and discuss the power of silence
Mother Earth returns to her rightful role as goddess
I dream of this day

I dream of the day coffee is a free commodity, gasoline is non-existent
Love is traded on the stock market, corporations are not people
Television has no agenda, entertainment is thought-provoking
Internet is sewn into our fingers, starvation is non-existent
Disease is no longer our fate, and cancer has a cause

I dream of the day you and I continue on without end
You and I touch without physical interaction
You and I find ourselves inseparable
Welcome everywhere, any time

I dream of the day harmony takes form
Synchronicity is finally achieved
I dream of the day we follow our chi
Find the tao inside every living thing

I dream of the day we have nothing left to dream of
Because every day, every moment
We be just as we should

A fantasy without limitation
A reality beyond imagining

POETRY COPTER

Let's get one thing straight

I don't like miscommunication
I don't like misunderstanding
And I don't appreciate you assuming
I like doing this poetry thing

It's a labor of lust

I don't do it for anyone but me
Still, I get the feeling you get me
You get something from it
You get it

A fleeting feeling
A newfound thought
A deeper wound
A tighter stomp

I know what you're thinking, you're thinking
"He does this for the riches"
But no
I do poetry because
It itches the inside of my skull
All day, every day, and
I can't get away from myself
Long enough
It's hell

Might fly off the shelves
Tomorrow
Might be on the black market
Today

I could care less

When it's bad, it's good
When it's worse, it's even better
When it's left unwritten, it's best

Don't ever get mistaken
Ink never forgets

While my mind decides the next line it's set to write
I sit here in a coffee shop early in the morning
Asking myself

Where have I gone?
Where have I come from?
How do I plan on getting back?
Why would I ever want to?

Let's get one thing straight
I didn't choose to start writing poetry
Poetry chose to ride with me

I often wonder
What was poetry thinking?

I question its credibility

SWING

I see you got that something in your eye, child
But one day, you better realize you still got that hook
Because you look at where you're jabbing, but blabbing
I'm still standing right here in front of you

I wanna see what you're made of

In the ring, the whites of your eyes have gone red
Breathing heavily, head held high, you're not yet dead
Still, you got both your dukes up in front of your face
Hiding the disgrace of too many punches thrown
And a whole lot of nothing landed

So now, it's time to change it up a bit
Maybe deviate from what'cha been up'ta
It's time to shake it up a bit, maybe
See what it is you're made of

Because if you quit now
You're just gonna be down and out, and
Right now, you've got the fight of your life
Standing right here in front of you
And truth be told
Every underdog gets themselves there somehow

So what do you say?
You gonna go ahead and let me make my day
Or are you gonna do something, anything about it
To bring about some change?
Create your own fate?

I wanna know

Because if you're still standing
You've got more than you would
From down there on the floor

Go ahead

Swing

Kiss Me (Between Blinking)

Kiss me
Again
With that
Look

I know
You've got
That look
In you

When eyes
Meet eyes
Or lips
Meet lips
It is
A kiss
One cannot
Envisage

One can
Only fashion
Such things
Through
Union

Prove to me
Right here
Right now
That light
In you
Shining
When I
Find you
Inside
Yourself
Is real

Prove me
Right

Kiss me
Again

With that
One look

I wouldn't mind

Appears
Your looks
Could kill
If warranted

Kiss me
Kill me
Whatever
You do
Don't leave
Me breathing

You've
Got
Sex
In you

You've got
Me in you

Don't look now

I've got
You in
Me too

And then
We blink
Without
Goodbye

Speak to Me

Speak to me in words
Words I have never heard before
Before I ever met you here
Here in real life

I find everyone singing noise
Noise with no substance, no truth
Truth beyond a reasonable doubt
Doubt full of sounds screamed aloud

Believe me, I was only sleeping
Dreaming of a life within your love
Trusting the winds and where they send us
Bound to weightlessness
Completely

Compassion in our shoulders
Light in the soles of our feet
A smile in our bellies
Mind teeming with potential
And a song inside our seat

Speak to me
In words
I have never
Heard before

Your voice
Will be
The life
Of me

Why I Can't Wake Up at Six in the Morning

If I do
The evil monsters will get me

If I do
World peace will continue
To not exist

If I wake up at six in the morning
The universe collapses

That's a warning you can take to the grave
I wouldn't let me sleep in on it

I can stay up
Until 6 in the morning

I can stir at 6 in the morning
Only to hit snooze
But never shall I awake
At 6 a.m.

If I do
The Mayans
Will have been right
The entire time

Don't let me catch the worm
I've got zzz's to chase down

If I don't
This bus will explode

Give me just another few minutes of fuse to burn

I don't want to sleep through
Destroying the world

Imagine

Last Takeoff

It's like they knew we were going to die

They aren't usually overly charismatic
Telling us the safety information before takeoff
But this time seemed a little more like
Why even bother?

Once we took off
I had a funny feeling about this flight
I say so to myself every time we launch into the sky
But this has never before felt so right

We hit ten-thousand feet
The electronic device light turned off
The seat belt sign stayed on
Then, all of a sudden, just silence

Terminal velocity on every side
Nose diving to the end of our lives
In slow motion, faster than any of us has ever fallen
We were all sullen in our descent

The oxygen masks never fell
Our life preservers were no good
The crew continued serving drinks and food
And I simply kept writing poetry

It's all that I could do

Untitled (Re-Vision)

I devise, I rewrite
Tear it apart, then
Start all over again

I find I go
Nowhere fast
Often easily

Caught up in my mind
Indecisive by design, I try
To find direction for no destination
An electron lost amongst the equation

How does one know
What they are looking for
When their quest is
Undefined; an answer
Man made as time

I devise, I rewrite
Tear it apart, then
Make it right

To do better
No matter
Rising above
The letter of grammar

Always tomorrow
A new man
Revised

I am
Far
From
Finished

To My Unborn Wonder

Dear unborn
Son or daughter

I eagerly await
The moment I meet you

Before you're old enough
To become disenfranchised
Please, remember this
In no particular order

Be yourself
You don't owe anyone anything, besides yourself
Speak your mind
Embrace the silence and chaos that surround you
Listen passionately
Dream emphatically
Entertain time-tested wisdom as if it were new-fangled fashion
Question mediocrity
Take at least one deep breath hourly
Discover your center
Learn from every mistake
Take chances by the throat
Find God
Trust your instincts
Go with the flow
Love your family, humanity
Denounce discrimination
Weed the garden of your mind
Nurture your spirit
Meditate once in a while
Drink lots of water
Enjoy the little things
Act as if all moments are perfect
Kiss your crush
Marry your soul mate
Sing, dance, and fuck fast, loud, and safely
Practice daily life without restraint
Deviate from preconceived notions
Let no one stop you from destiny
Be the change, for better or worse
Invest time in good karma

Desire nothing
Peace comes from within
Respect posture
Hold the future hostage
Appreciate nature
Go ask your mother
Take your time
Optimism is your greatest ally
Sleep is an illusion
Culture is the enemy
I will let you down at times
Experiment with daily life
Follow your gut
Everything's negotiable
Celebrate your youth while you can
You're going to go to college; start planning now
If you make a promise, keep it
Hard work pays off
Age is not a curse
Nature above all else
Don't look back
Don't let anyone else carry your flag
Second chances are not guaranteed
Always choose love

Please remember this
Before you become disenfranchised
By the world-at-large

I love you

And there's nothing
You can do about it

See you soon

Love is/in Life
By Sean Hill

(We are) Be(autiful)

Seeing Circles

Living Circles

Movements

Arguments Are Shoelaces

Light (Coach) Love

I'm Sorry (And I don't Feel Bad About It)

Supernova Battle Cry

I'm Only Human

Enjoy ~ Breathe ~ Share ~ Dialogue ~ Grow ~ Feel ~ Thanks

(We are) Be(autiful)

Loving life living light
living life lighter than a feather
leave no trace
but tracks of love
sharing smiles
like show and tell is everyday
duck duck goose
kind of laughter
playing games of moments
where there is no after
no leftovers
having seconds of time
delicious
wishing everyone can taste

what's funny
is everyone can make it
passion everlasting

remembering dreams
from a lovely rest
wake up
another fun test
another way to live life better than best
another day to pay it for-word
for free, so easy
keeping every word like promises
then let it be
letting go of who we thought we were
get a tiny brief buzz of who we can be
sifting out what we don't want
accepting what we do when it comes through
hard work feels beautiful
determination feels beautiful
this journey feels beautiful
you feel beautiful
you feel beautiful
feel beautiful
feel beautiful
so
beautiful

Seeing Circles

Every Lion King
started as a kitten prince
every adventurer
had to learn home wasn't a picket fence
every lover
had to mend their heart with self made stitches
so whenever I hit hard places
leaving my head spinning in circles
I take time to rewind life
pause on moments that help əm/me reflect
stop living in circles that don't complete me
play in every circle that leaves me whole
fast forward through regrets
remembering every frame
is named with possibility
so why would I live in indecisive slow-motion
when I can love every scene at organic speed

they say you can't tell when a circle begins
or ends, but my friend …
I can tell you

any circle starts

when you become a part of it
any circle ends

when you walk out of it

head high
heart in hand
feeling free to fly
knowing now
forever
how
to land

Living Circles

I knew a little lady once
lovely little light
she had the voice of a righteous queen
an angel with new wings,
effortless beauty to listen to each night
she would sing at this open mic
I asked her one time
what she wants to do with her life
she said, I don't know
I feel like I'm stuck in a circle
Why is that, I asked
surprised to see stagnation in her eye
she said her mom always wanted to sing
professionally she said it wasn't possible
so her daughter should do no such thing
too big of an obstacle
mentally, I could see she already settled

I told her, Look
whatever mistakes she did
aren't the ones you have to make
life isn't decided for us
as much as the risks we take
some people awake each day
thinking life lives them
in fact looking back, we live life
so when wrong feels right
know you've settled for less
then just do what you love for one day
see how you feel
if you don't have time
make time
because it's less time
you'll spend in the future
turning purple
from not breathing your dreams
going from home, work, work to
home is where your heart is
where your garden is
planting seeds of love and focus
is strength tilling daily
in the soil of your atoms

just remember to go on
keep assertive
best way to live free
create your own
circle

she smiled
hid her eyes
from letting me see
the connecting truth
she feels
checking if she is done
with this conversation

she said thanks for taking the time
the patience to speak with me

I said, Hey
what else are we here for
              our eyes swim
if not each other
                they step out the ocean
we smile
we walked away

Movements

I want to be
m   o   v   e   d

I used to be glued
to this setting silicone sun
fun was had by how bad a movie was
hearing stories
of how love was made just because

rhyme and reason were partners in crime
thought these times were sublime
but I found out
they weren't truly mine
I was grooving
to other people's tunes in life
carpooling

in someone else's belief system

not seeing my self
in the world's definitions
checking a thesaurus for "self"
made by the same creator
of dictionaries
never knowing my own sound
in the world's stereo
surrounding me

I've been an inner child
abandoned, starving
to be moved

hun-gry-t-o fe-el-con-nect-ed
li-ving to do more than pay the next b-ill

seeing through any temporary thrill
my cup always half filled
avalanche rushing

now I'm
living to be
        still

Arguments Are Shoelaces

Two hands tugging

pulling

at the same piece of string

trying to do

the same thing

achieve the same goal

pulling

constantly

struggling

different

angles

always believing

their part of string

deserves to be looped first

driving each other

knots

forgetting

at important times

they are forever connected

to the same

source

holding on

to different points

oh

if they could just let go

let their place go

understand

the dance

beginning

the mingling

of string

ending

either first or last ring

to close the loop

rest secure

the other

was always just trying

to hold the other tightly

lovingly
close

to their
same

sole

Light (Coach) Love

"I just got inspired to make you a delicious sandwich"

Yeah

she says things like that

matters and facts
get less meaningful
when she shoots me with straight truth
loots my brain of mind
so I'm outta my head
quicker than ever
whenever she's around
she looks at me
like
I
wish a woman
would look at me
so I guess
she makes my wishes
come true
she's sincere and silly
but with such confidence
in her love of me
in her faith in me
in her love of this world
this universe
isn't big enough
to hold her love
and dreams
lovely dreams
that whisper
beauty into every ear
that hears them
or bears witness
bears are witnesses
to how much she loves nature
naturally she loves learning
she memorizes happiness
speaks the language of love
fluently, bisexual with honesty
and understanding

our threeways are amazing
talking about anything
everything we've experienced
we think have made us ready
for the truthiest love possible
the love that wants what's best
for the other
but doesn't need to enforce it
the love that is free to be
loves individual choices
the love that enjoys the other
but doesn't depend on
we thrive
nicely knowing
loving
that each other
exists

I'm Sorry (And I Don't Feel Bad About It)

I
Am
Sorry.

Three magic words
that require no genie

three words
that are more than words

three words
that so many
are deathly afraid to say

oh, apologies …

why are you so tricky …

people want you
only when they need you
yet they don't realize
how good you feel

going in us
and coming out

seriously Sorrys …
I gotta tell ya …
you're frickin' amazing

you have the power
to relieve guilt
empower forgiveness
all while
barely needing to be said above a whisper

so many never know
that you don't need to be yelled out ever …
you actually lose your effect
when that happens
when you are said
with anything less than love

or more than patience ...

well, you just wouldn't be the same.

people say you without meaning it
and we all can see it

Sorry ...
I am so sorry
that we aren't sorry enough

That we think when we are sorry
we have to feel guilt ...

when in fact
we're supposed to feel free

free from the guilt of what we did wrong
and after letting the guilt go ...

we never need to feel guilty
anymore when we say it ...

Sorry ...
can now be
the best way to say
that you acknowledge
you could have done something better

let's let go of the guilt trips
we all have packed bags enough
to go on them way too much

we are now ...
in a new age
of sorry ...
better than the board game ...

a new vacation
can now take place

we can leave pain forever ...
and never come back

we can say Sorry

and truly mean it

we can say Sorry
and feel happy
when we say it

we can say Sorry
and say it genuinely
just for the other person

one man said
don't be Sorry
be joyous
instead

we can say it

for all the inner children
of our student body
so they can learn
the truth
about saying sorry
and grow stronger
no longer
carrying backpacks of guilt
but keeping their books of intelligent
emotional freedom
filled with blank notepads of closure
3 ring binders with
pages of peace
spilling out
beautifully
now saying sorry
with the biggest smile
and heart
to match

Supernova Battle Cry

War

is inspirational

proudly patriotic
our duty
a must
a necessary evil
a justified attack
a way of the world
no other route

until you find out

how mothers

have the best battle cries

      when a sun dies

sometimes
not enough pieces of them
left to ship home

a black hole
endlessly creating itself in parents
hearts

believing war
is necessary
to bring peace

is thinking
drowning
necessary

to breathe air

we teach our children
to solve problems
and misunderstandings
through dialogue

compromise
the sacrifice
of pride

but as adults
we send the same children
to wars
we built them weapons
to fight for
ideals we all
don't
really
believe
in
a last resort?
no other way?
self defense?
freedom?
this is just how it is …?

the greatest untold battles
are fought in our hearts
and minds not taking the time
to truly apply a new solution
has become a tired tale
we no longer fall asleep

we have practiced more patience
to hate ourselves in wars
than develop love for someone else

which we can change

by rearranging our priorities
of which book we want to read first
from off our shelves:

the Book of Last Resorts
is better to read if we plan vacations

the Book of No Other Way
is really a lazy read for not trying harder
or applying perspective

the Book of Self Defense

has been more of a stubborn belief
that our life is more important than another
because "they" have a different culture
we don't fully understand and this book
is based on a true story historically

I see the last book we often read

the Book of Freedom

… this old shelf holding this old story …

we think these are self help books
they turn out to be self
hurt

establishing freedom
by killing in wars
is an arranged marriage attitude
hoping what we put in place
is the best for both parties
without fully knowing and caring
who and what they want
within

within
we can begin
to stop these wars

weapons fall
when hearts think

then suns will rise
our souls will blink

we can't fight
if there are no soldiers
or believers of war
on either side

when soldiers decide
it is better to live for their ideals
than die for their country
who made their ideals
dying for their country

dying for our country
is in fact hurting our country
by taking away our precious lives
fracturing our lovely families
minusing a father-mother
sister-brother all the same
in the name of "honor"
but not
in integrity
to know why we fight
to know the history of who we are
before the end of this book
find out what it means
to be human

we can choose
to help our human leaders
who make mistakes
like the rest of us
figure things out
by standing down
sitting down
and enjoying a show together

make some art
that will heal wounds
so much sooner
than making new ones
believe me
it works
I've seen it
heard it, felt it
read it
the works of people
war torn who mend themselves
in the silence and peace
of reading, understanding poetry
peace on a canvas
peace in writing
peace on that big screen
peace in creating a theater scene
peace in writing a story
peace in making laughter
peace in making peace inside
putting together pieces

that we thought we could hide
with bombs and bullets
thought we could stuff
good intentions
inside
ammunition
but really inside us
inside all of us
that believe in war

there is a bomb
we
can dismantle

there is a bullet
we
don't need to fire

there is a fire
we
don't ever need to set

I don't know
exactly what will happen
when we push reset

but I do know
it is the best step
towards the direction of love
real love
for each other
ourselves
real self reflection
of the complaints we are cancered
of saying

and beautiful
realistic world peace
will be ours
for the making
ours for the creating
ours for the enjoying

and finally

we can put an end
to creating black holes
in the hearts of parents

we can start keeping our new dawns
our new suns

burning their light fiery
spinning true

keeping our
soular systems
aligned lovely
brightly alive

I'm Only Human

I'm

only

human

I'm

only

infinite .

I'm only connected
to a collective consciousness
of an entire species
who thrives to exist

I'm only connected to a source
known and unknown
that is forever
creates
answers us
in mysterious and all loving ways

I'm only human

I'm only a single part of a whole

I'm only a single universe of atoms

I'm only DNA directly affected
culminating to the current vibration
combination of chromosomes
testosterone, estrogen, electricity,
H2O and more

I'm only human
having a consciousness
as large as my imagination
creating illusions
as real as blueprints

to buildings until manifested
as constructed concepts
become tangible

My imagination
is impossibly
perfect

Designed to envision
I have visions
that can give stress
or give alternate scenarios to test
while calling my body to react
like imagining drowning
could make me short of breath
while the image of myself in bed
with a love that has the self confidence
of a lion
with the heart of a penguin
could make my heart skip a beat, a lung
or a decade

I'm only human

With a capacity of love
that can make each breath I take
feel like it matters
to make matters worse
it makes it feel like I matter
to someone else
with a wealth inside
that feels like diamonds
died compared to this feeling
of bliss from a kiss that was free
to give
to receive
honestly

Human

from Pangaea to now
we are one
with determination
discipline
infinite gifts

to confront our grief
ignorance & suffering
to completely face
the worst in ourselves
throughout our history
still see through any misery
beyond bending reality
confidently connecting new synapses
creating new habits
to progress and change
process then remain
together
unified
keep going on as lovingly
as possible through all
previous obstacles

It seems

                                                        the best thing

we could ever

say

                                                                            is

                          I'm
                         only
                        human

About the Authors

Photo by Kris Rubio

Jason Brain

A lifelong native Angeleno, Jason Brain's favorite hobby is breathing. When he's not breathing, Jason is an unapologetic Spoken Word Poet and creative arts advocate. His 1st published collection of poetry, <u>Mix Tape Collection I: Original Poetry</u>, is available worldwide on Amazon.com.

Jason is also a theatric playwright; visual artist focused in photography and sacred geometry; and the founder of Soapbox International, an artistic community organization dedicated to encouraging creativity and empowering artists through its flagship open mic night, Soapbox Sessions.

He has recently started his own creative management company, focused on media marketing and business development, called Imagine Nation Agency.

Jason also enjoys making time for sports, meditation, and the little things in life (like beautiful sunsets, good friends, and delicious coffee) between it all.

He hopes to meet you soon.

www.JasonBrain360.com
www.SPBX.org

About the Authors

Photo by Kris Rubio

C.R. Cohen

Chelsea Rose Cohen's love affair with words, cinema and the arts has lead her to many fulfilling places on her creative journey: owning and operating a film production company, teaching creative writing and film, and enjoying the release of her first book of poetry, *Beatnik Femme Fatale* on Amazon.com.

An arts activist at heart, Chelsea founded Artists Underground in 2010, a creative community offering valuable networking, resources and knowledge to artists through collaborative events and its website, artists-underground.com. Her weekly Well Fed Artist blog is featured on Soapbox Radio on BlogTalkRadio.com.

After four years as a business and financial manager, Chelsea left to pursue her twin passions for writing and talent development. She has joined Imagine Nation Agency as a manager and consultant for emerging artists and will be completing her first novel, *Jenny With The Sound Turned Down* in 2014. In the last quarter of 2013, she placed 2nd in the International Indi.com Poetry Slam Competition with her performance of *Dream Zombie* written earlier that year.

In her spare time, she listens to jazz and Sinatra while drinking goblets of red wine and chopping and searing things in the kitchen. She is forever plotting her escape up the coast to San Francisco, but will settle for now with the beautiful life she has here in LA.

www.beatnikfemmefatale.com
www.artists-underground.com

About the Authors

Photo by Kris Rubio

Sean Hill

Living for 8 months in Beijing studying while performing Theater deeply impacted and enhanced the passion of living Sean Hill wishes to share with the world. His artistry embraces all people while reminding them of why we are beautifully fun beings regardless of what we go through or what we confront inside or out.

He is highly influenced by his family and parents who made putting 5 kids through college & going through 3 types of cancer look easy. Relatives, past/present: he is grateful beyond measure for "youse" from CA, NY, Colombia, St. Kitts to Pangea. His lover who supports & encourages him with her light, even when he gets used to the dark, a wonder of beautiful combinations of being. Also, a recycler of inspiration from his friends, teachers & favorite artists from Whitman to Denzel, Ellen to Plato: they have made this world & life easier.

He features at festivals across the U.S., has shared the stage with Diplo/Big Sean, David & Devine, Andy Grammer and more, hosts events for youth homes & high schools. He tours with *The Ki* ("Energy" in Japanese) a musical ensemble & movement. He is a SAG actor, released his first spoken word album in 2012 while hosting & performing at open mics at colleges and teaching afterschool poetry/theater. He promotes wholeheartedly the Emblem 3 youth project, *Team Inspire*, Doctors Without Borders, National Animal Rights Day, ChrisBeatCancer.com, & the UN Women Greater Los Angeles Chapter.

He will leave this world much better than he was fortunate enough to enter it.

www.reverbnation.com/seanraymondhill

Previously Published Poems:

C.R. Cohen

"Moth to Flame"
1st published Spring 2013
In The Words of Womyn chapbook by ITWOW California

"Beatnik Femme Fatale III"
1st published November 2011
Beatnik Femme Fatale by C.R. Cohen on CreateSpace

Also by **Poetry in Motion Publishing House**:

Mix Tape Collection: Original Poetry by Jason Brain
Poetry In Motion Publishing House, 2012

www.ingramcontent.com/pod-product-compliance
Lightning Source LLC
LaVergne TN
LVHW041546070426
835507LV00011B/948